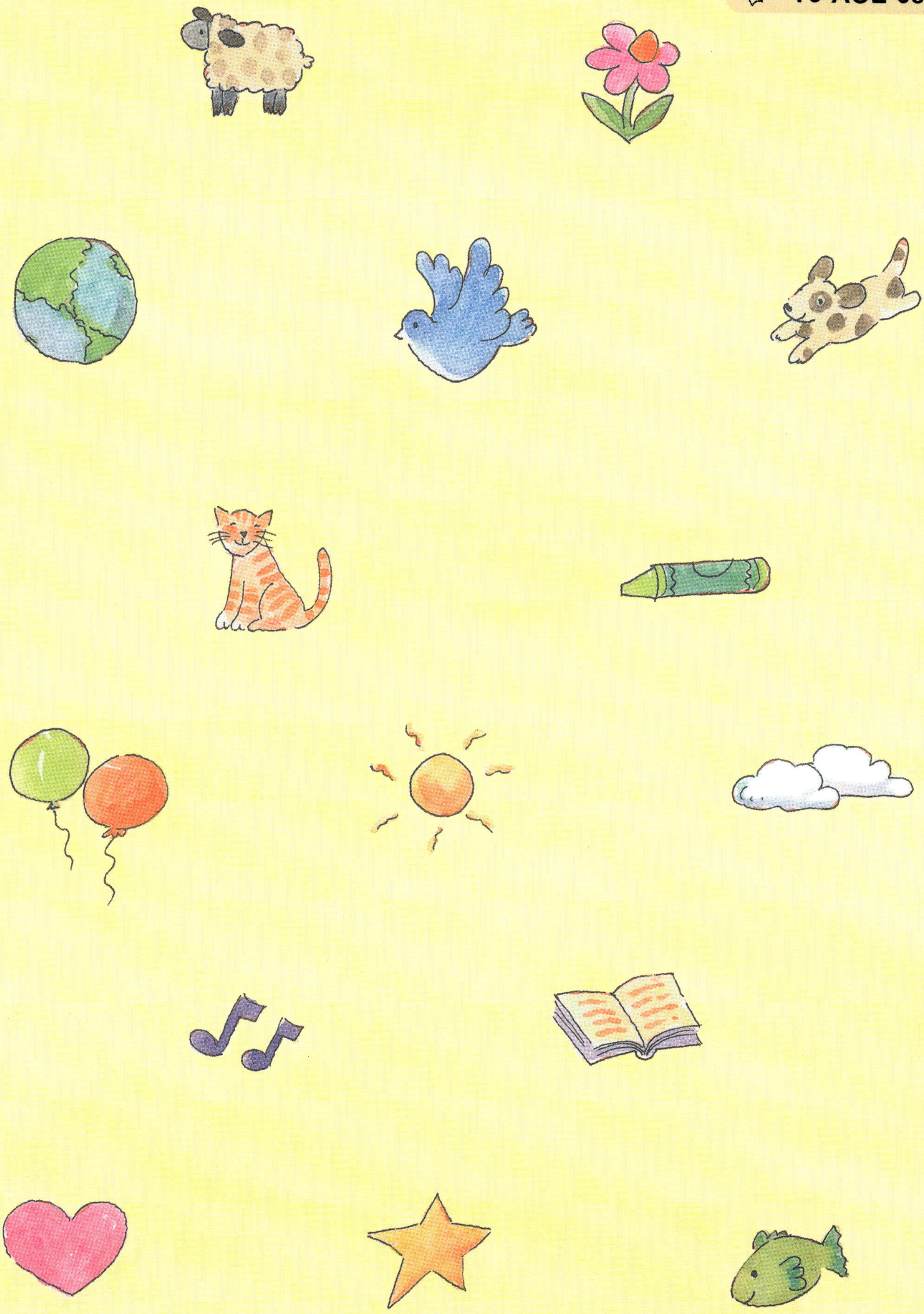

the Bible and Me

A Keepsake Book

I am

_____

This book was presented

_____

by

_____

on

_____

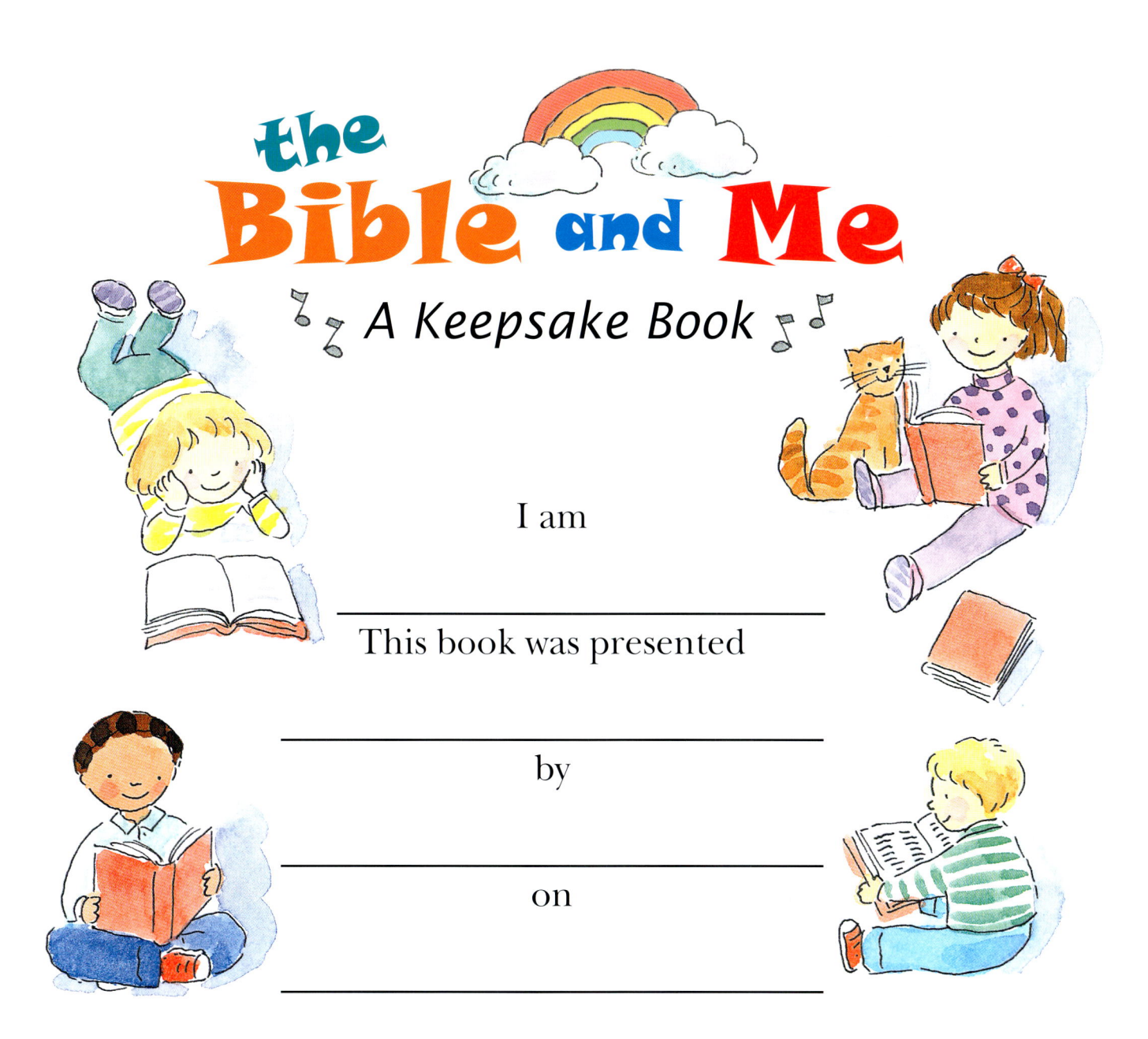

Rebecca A. Egbert with pictures by Shelley Dieterichs

CPH
Concordia Publishing House

Me

My name is

_____.

I am _____ years old.

My birthday is

_____.

just-for-fun

I will paste

a picture

of me here.

I am _____ feet and _____ inches tall.

I wear a size _____ shoe.

just-for-fun

I will take off my shoes and socks and trace my feet here.

just-for-fun

I will
☐ draw a picture of my family here

☐ paste a picture of my family here

Just-for-Fun

I do lots of fun things.
I like to

- ☐ read books
- ☐ eat ice cream
- ☐ play soccer
- ☐ do homework
- ☐ create masterpieces
- ☐ go to the zoo

My Bible

I have a very special Book!

The name of my book is the Holy Bible.
Do you know who wrote the Holy Bible?
God did! Now you know why it is so special.
And guess what?
Every story in the Bible is true.
I like my Bible!

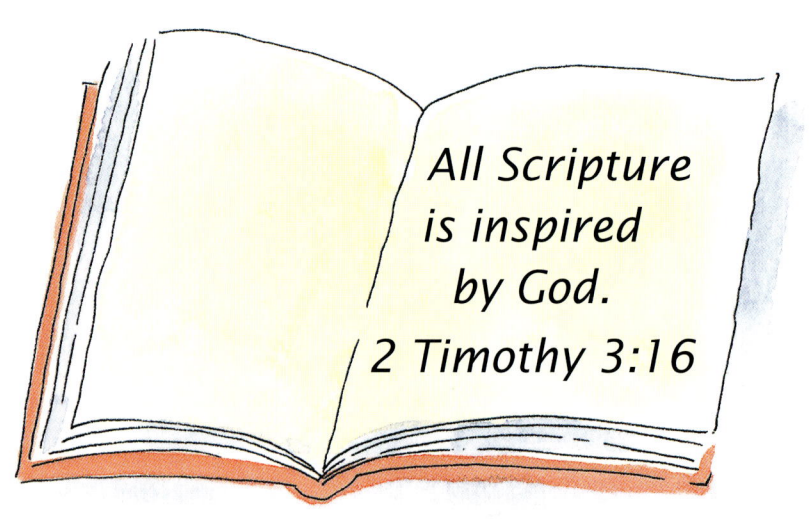

All Scripture is inspired by God.
2 Timothy 3:16

Just-for-Fun

☐ I will paste a picture of me with my Bible here.

☐ I will draw a picture of my Bible here.

☐ I will sing the song "The B-I-B-L-E."
(Your Sunday school teacher might be able to help you sing this song.)

God the Father

God tells me about Himself in the Bible.
Did you know God made the whole world?
He did!

God tells us in the B__ __ __ __
that He made the world in seven days.
Wow! God really worked fast.
I wonder if it was easy for Him
to make the whole world in seven days?

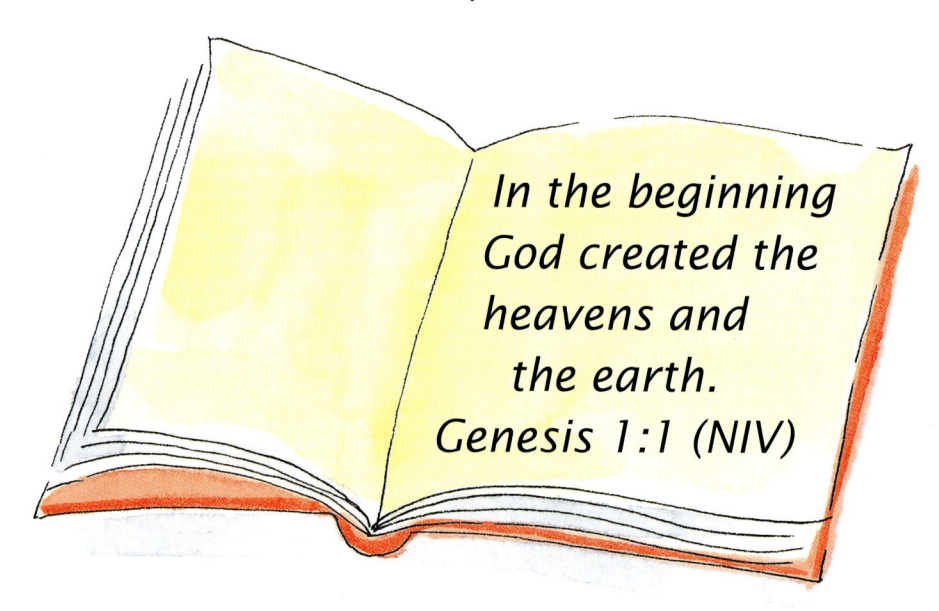

*In the beginning God created the heavens and the earth.
Genesis 1:1 (NIV)*

just-for-Fun I will write the numbers
1, 2, 3, 4, 5, 6, and 7
in the boxes.

In the middle, I will draw a picture of God's world.

God made everything in the world in seven days. He really did!

My B__ __ __ __ says He did!

This is the way God created the world:

On day 1, God made day and night.

On day 2, God made the sky.

On day 3, God made the land, oceans, trees, bushes, plants, and grass.

On day 4, God made the sun, the moon, and the stars.

just-for-fun
I will draw a picture of the things God made on each day.

Day 1

Day 2

Day 3

Day 4

On day 5, God made the fish and the birds. Wow! God was really busy.

just-for-fun

I will count the birds in this picture.

My favorite bird is _____.

So God created the great creatures of the sea ... and every winged bird.
Genesis 1:21 (NIV)

On day 6, God created the animals.
I will name the animals.

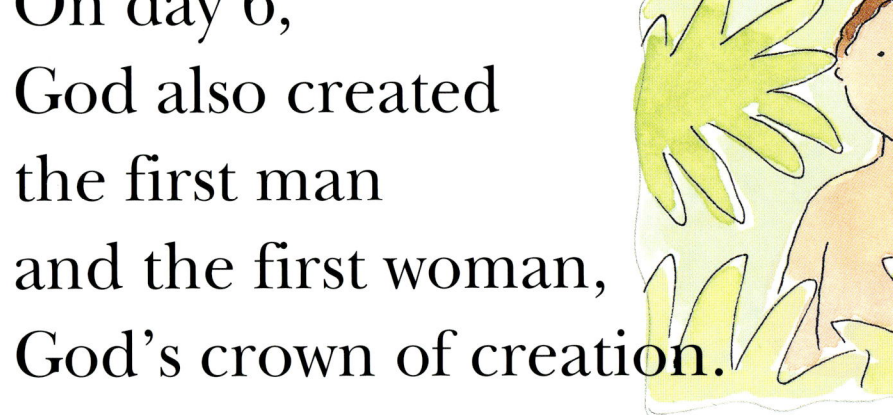

On day 6,
God also created
the first man
and the first woman,
God's crown of creation.

The man was named
_____.

The woman was
named _____.
(See Genesis 3:20 for the answers.)

God told them to take care of His world
and to have children.

just-for-fun

I will draw a picture
of the first people.

On day 7, God rested.
Wow! I wonder if God was tired?

just-for-fun

I will draw
a circle around
my favorite things
that God made.

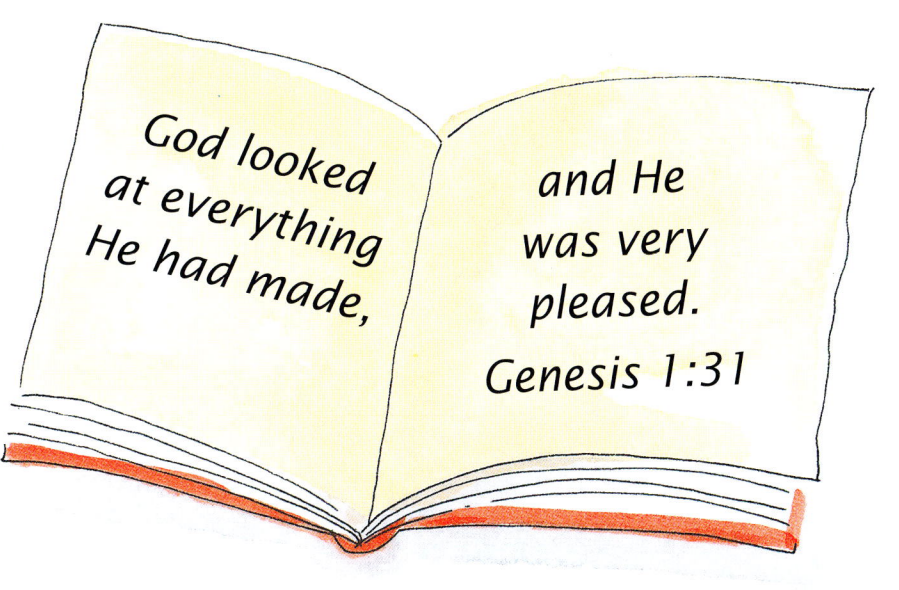

God looked at everything He had made, and He was very pleased.
Genesis 1:31

God's Promises

One day Adam and Eve disobeyed God.
They had to leave the beautiful garden.
God still loved them.
God gave them a promise.
He promised to send a Savior.

just-for-Fun I will color the hearts.

After many years, some people stopped obeying God.
God sent a flood to destroy the earth, but God saved
Noah and his family because they were faithful.
God gave them a promise.
God sent a rainbow to show that He keeps His promises.

just-for-Fun

I will draw a rainbow.
I will use these colors:
red, orange, yellow, green, blue, purple

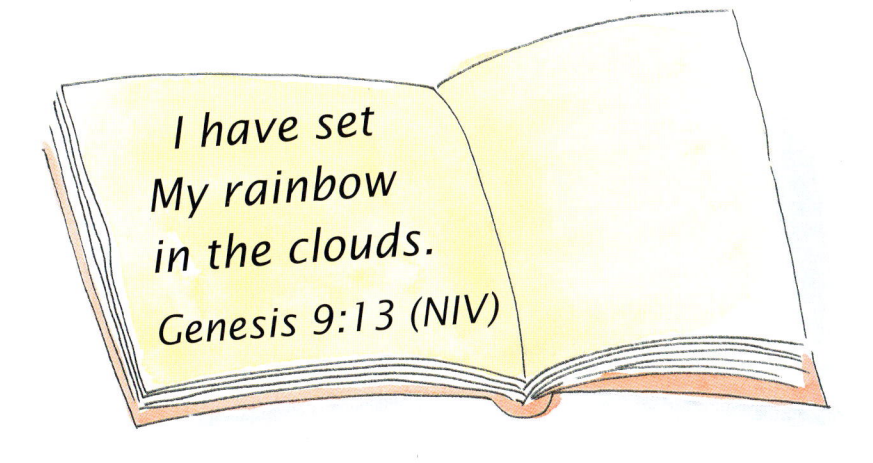

> I have set
> My rainbow
> in the clouds.
> Genesis 9:13 (NIV)

God's Chosen People

My B__ __ __ __ tells me God gave a special blessing to a man named Abraham.

God told Abraham he would be the father of many nations.

Abraham had a son named __ __ __ __ __.
(Genesis 21:1–3)

Isaac had a son named __ __ __ __ __.
(Genesis 25:24–26)

And Jacob had _____ sons. (Genesis 35:22)

These families were called the children of Israel, God's chosen people.

just-for-Fun

I will sing "Father Abraham."
(Your Sunday school teacher might be able to help you sing this song.)

> You are the people that I have chosen, the descendants of Abraham, My friend.
> Isaiah 41:8

just~for~Fun

I will
- ☐ paste a picture of my family here
- ☐ draw a picture of my family here

The children of Israel became slaves in Egypt.
They had to work very hard.

God chose a man named __ __ __ __ __ to rescue
His people (Exodus 3:1–10).

But the children of Israel disobeyed God.
God punished them, but He still loved them.
God would keep His promise to send a Savior.

just-for-Fun

I will mark the face that shows
how I feel because I know God loves me
and sent a Savior for me too.

My B __ __ __ __ tells me about God and the wonderful things He made.

My Bible tells me what happens when God's people disobey.

It tells me God keeps His promises.

Best of all, my Bible tells me about God's promise to send a Savior.

It tells me about Jesus!

My B __ __ __ __ is wonderful!

just-for-Fun

I will decorate the bookmark in the Bible.

Yes, my B __ __ __ __
tells me about Jesus.

Jesus is my Savior.

Jesus is God's Son.

He really is!

My B __ __ __ __ tells me so.

Jesus was with God when He created the world.

He has been with God forever.

Jesus lives in heaven.

I live on earth.

My address is:

_____

_____

_____

Does Jesus have an address?

just~for~Fun I will write a letter to Jesus.

To Jesus
   In Heaven

Dear Jesus,

Your friend,

God the Son

Jesus is God's Son, and He came to earth to be my Savior. He became a tiny baby. His mother's name was Mary. An angel told Mary she would be the mother of God's Son. Was she ever surprised!

You will ... give birth to a Son, and you will name Him Jesus. Luke 1:31

just~for~Fun

I will connect the dots.

J__ __ __ __ was born
in a stable in Bethlehem.
(Luke 2:7)

This very day ...
your Savior
was born—
Christ the Lord.

Luke 2:11 TLB

Angels sang that night.

Shepherds and the Wise Men
came to worship Jesus.

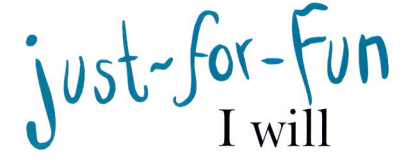

just-for-fun

I will
- ☐ make angels in the snow
- ☐ listen to the story of Jesus' birth in Luke 2:1–20
- ☐ sing "Away in a Manger"

Jesus grew up in a town called Nazareth.

Joseph was Jesus' father while He was here on earth.

Joseph was a carpenter, and Jesus was his helper.

just-for-Fun I will circle the things that are different in each picture.

Jesus learned many things that were in the Holy Scriptures.
(That's another name for God's Word.)
When Jesus was 12 years old, He visited the temple
in Jerusalem. The temple was the church where Jesus
and His earthly family worshiped God.

just-for-Fun

I will
- ☐ paste a picture
   of my church here
- ☐ draw a picture
   of my church here

The teachers in the temple read God's Word.
It was written on paper called scrolls.
The teachers were surprised to find out how much Jesus knew about God's Word.

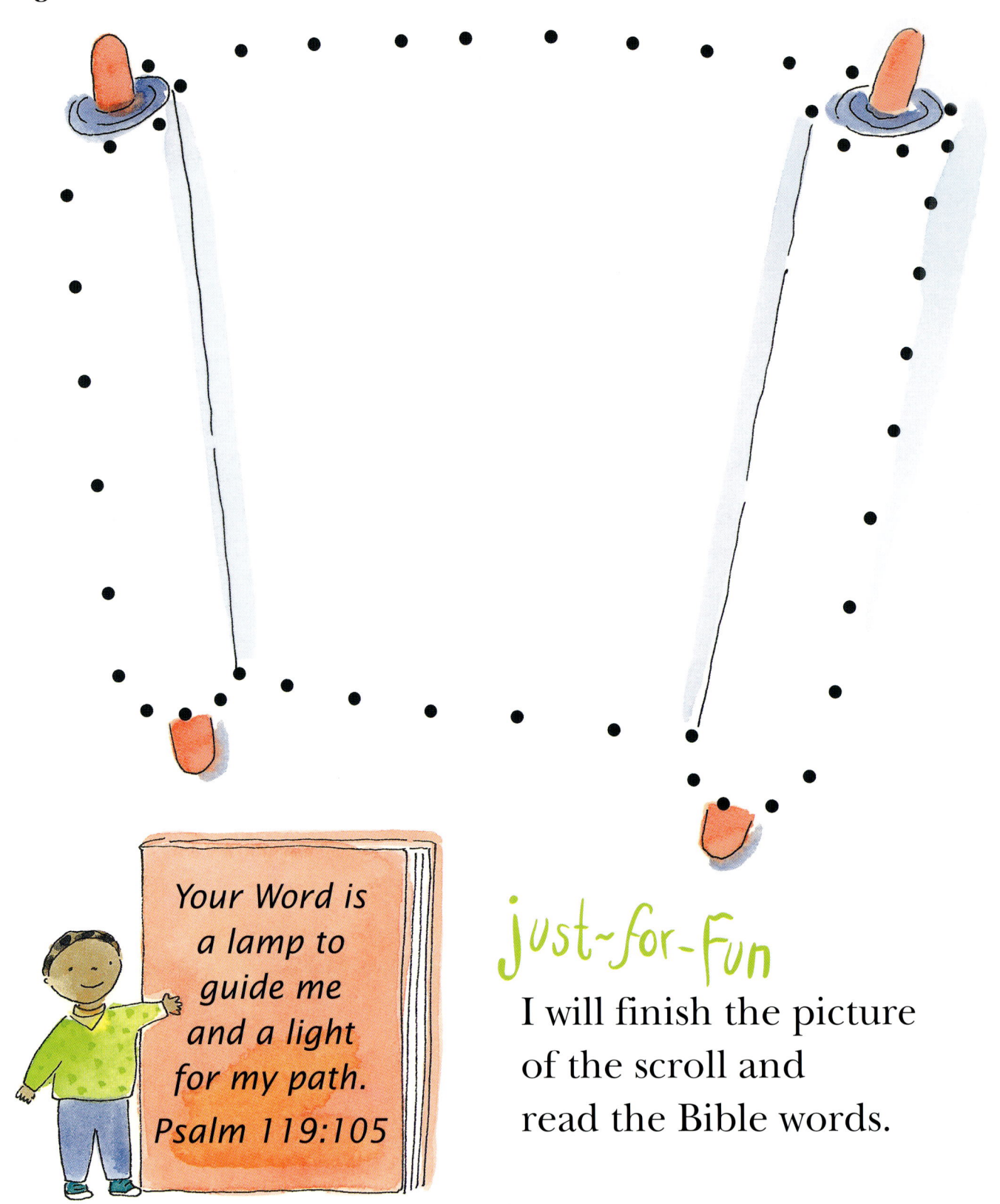

Your Word is a lamp to guide me and a light for my path.
Psalm 119:105

just-for-Fun

I will finish the picture of the scroll and read the Bible words.

When Jesus grew up, He did many miracles.

Did you know
He walked on water?
He did!
I wish I could do that.

Jesus fed more than 5,000 people with two fish and five small loaves of bread.

Jesus healed many who were sick with all kinds of diseases.
Mark 1:34

Jesus even made a storm stop!

He healed people who were blind, and deaf, and very sick.

Many people asked Jesus for help when they were sick.
I can ask Jesus to help me when I am sick.

Jesus has healed my
- ☐ sore throat
- ☐ skinned knees
- ☐ bee stings
- ☐ sore finger
- ☐ broken arm

My B __ __ __ __ says that Jesus is my Good Shepherd.
That means I am Jesus' little lamb.
He takes care of me!
I am so glad that Jesus is my Shepherd.

Just-for-Fun

I will draw a picture of me with Jesus, my Shepherd.

I am the Good Shepherd... I know My sheep and they know Me.

John 10:14–15

Jesus tells a story about a sheep who was lost.
The shepherd found the sheep and brought it back.

just-for-Fun

I will
- ☐ read the story in Matthew 15:1–7
- ☐ finish the maze and help the shepherd find his lost sheep

Jesus, My Savior

I call Jesus my Savior because He died on the cross for the forgiveness of my sins.

My sins are the wrong things I do.

Jesus saved me from punishment for my sins.

Because of Jesus, my sins are forgiven.

Jesus loves me, and I love Jesus!

just-for-Fun

I will color each empty square.

Breaking my toys

Calling someone a bad name

Helping a friend

Telling a lie

Sharing a treat

just-for-Fun
- ☐ I will draw a ✝ on the hearts that need forgiveness.
- ☐ I will draw a 🐟 on the hearts that show love.

Giving a hug

Obeying my parents

Hitting my friends

Jesus' friends were sad when He died.
But the friends of Jesus were happy when they discovered that Jesus did not stay dead.
On Easter morning, Jesus came out of the tomb!

Alleluia! Jesus was alive!

Alleluia! Jesus is alive today!

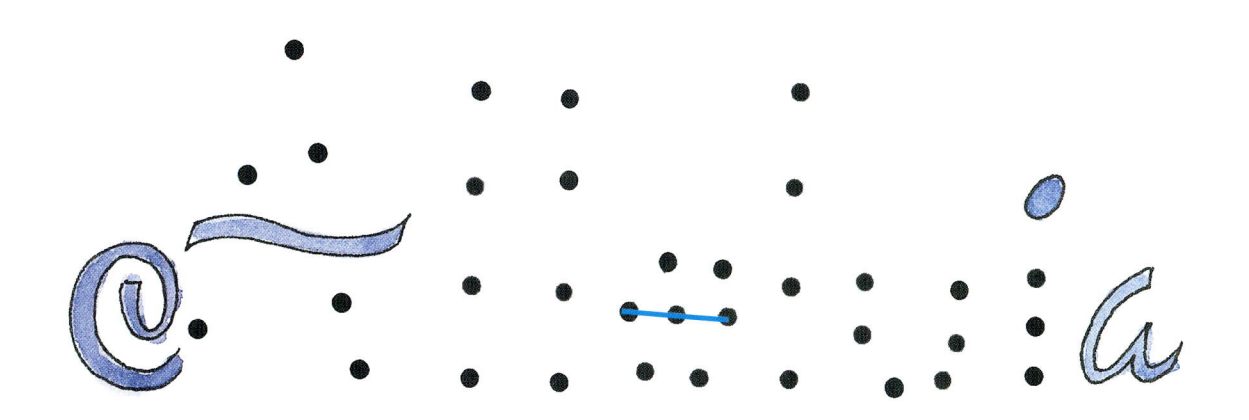

The Lord is risen indeed!
Luke 24:34

just-for-Fun
I will connect the dots to spell *ALLELUIA*.

Jesus came to see His friends many times after He came back to life.

One day, Jesus helped His friends catch a net full of fish.

He ate fish for breakfast with them.

just-for-fun
I will

☐ read the story in John 21:1–14

☐ draw lots of fish in the net

Jesus went back to heaven.
Before Jesus left, He made a promise.
He promised He would be with me always.

just-for-Fun

I will check the boxes that show when Jesus is with me.
Jesus is with me

☐ when I'm playing

☐ when I'm eating

☐ when I'm riding in a car

☐ when I'm at school

☐ when I'm sleeping

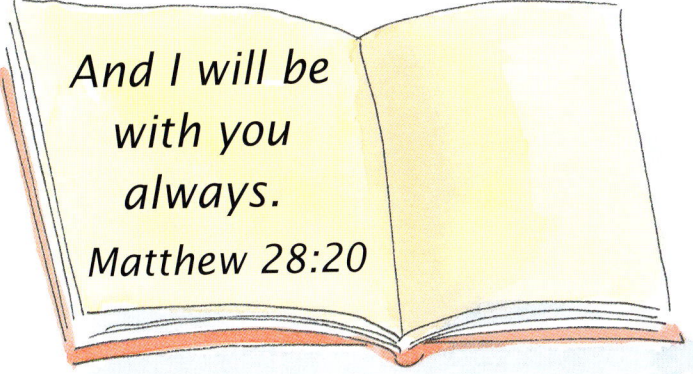

And I will be with you always.
Matthew 28:20

Jesus is preparing a place for me in heaven.
How do I know?
Because the Bible tells me so!

Because I believe that Jesus died for my sins and lives again, I will live forever in heaven.

Isn't Jesus wonderful?

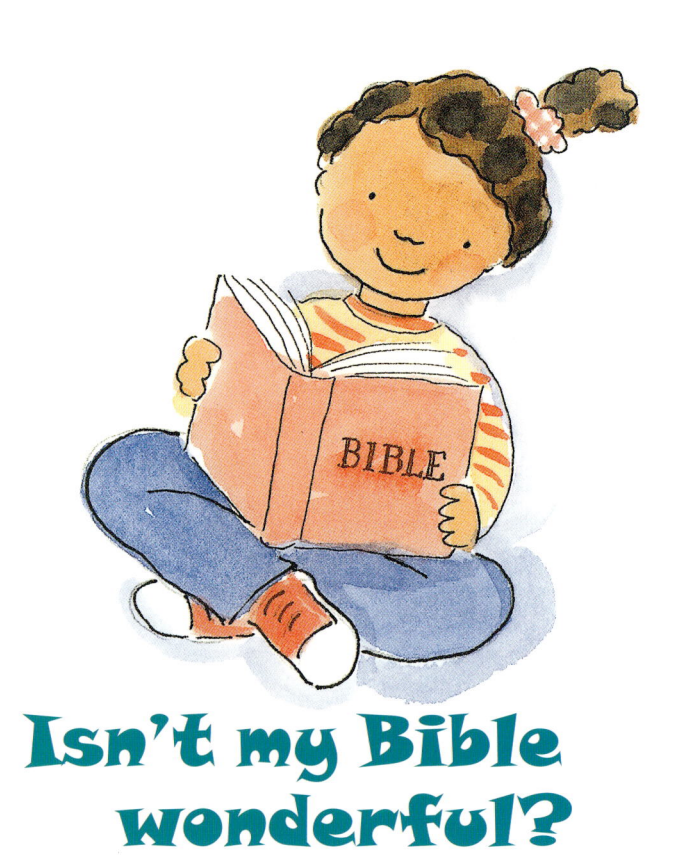

Isn't my Bible wonderful?

I will draw a picture just-for-fun of what I think heaven looks like.

God the Holy Spirit

Believing that Jesus died for me and lives again is called faith. The Holy Spirit puts faith in my heart and helps me believe.

I can plant a seed in the ground and help it grow.

just-for-Fun

I will draw a picture of something that grows from a seed.

I cannot plant faith in my own heart or help it to grow. The Holy Spirit puts faith in my heart and helps it grow through God's Word.

I will draw a picture of God's Word, the Bible.

He is the Spirit, who reveals the truth about God.

John 14:17

The Holy Spirit came down from heaven as a dove when Jesus was baptized in the Jordan River.

just-for-Fun
I will draw a picture of a dove.

As soon as Jesus came up out of the water, He saw heaven opening and the Spirit coming down on Him like a dove.

Mark 1:10

is a child of God

I am a child of God. The Holy Spirit plants faith in my heart through the water of Baptism and God's Word.

just-for-fun
I will
- ☐ write my name on the Baptism banner
- ☐ color a border around the Baptism banner

Jesus promised to send the Holy Spirit
to be with His followers after He went back to heaven.

The Holy Spirit came to them on the first Pentecost.

Jesus' friends heard a sound like wind.

They saw the Holy Spirit come as flames like fire
on top of their heads.

just-for-fun

I will draw flames of fire above the heads of the believers.

On the first Pentecost, the Holy Spirit helped the believers tell other people the Good News about Jesus and God's love.

The Holy Spirit helps me tell others about Jesus too.

just~for~Fun

I will draw a picture of someone whom I will tell about Jesus and God's love.

The Holy Spirit helps all believers have faith in Jesus.
I worship with other believers when I go to church.

just-for-fun
I will draw faces on the people who are worshiping in church.

I am so glad God gave me His Word in the

B__ __ __ __!

The Bible tells me about God the Father.
It tells me about God the Son.
It tells me about God the Holy Spirit.

just-for-fun

☐ I will write my favorite Bible verse.

_____

_____

_____

☐ I will write a special prayer to God.

Dear God,

In Jesus' name. Amen.

Parents!

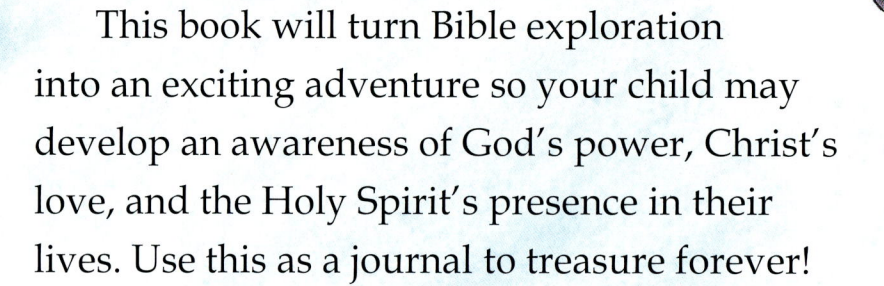

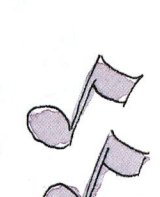

This book will turn Bible exploration into an exciting adventure so your child may develop an awareness of God's power, Christ's love, and the Holy Spirit's presence in their lives. Use this as a journal to treasure forever!

Scripture quotations, unless otherwise indicated, are taken from the Good News Bible, the Bible in TODAY'S ENGLISH VERSION. Copyright © American Bible Society, 1966, 1971, 1976. Used by permission.

Scripture quotations marked NIV are taken from the HOLY BIBLE, NEW INTERNATIONAL VERSION®. NIV®. Copyright © 1973, 1978, 1984 by International Bible Society. Used by permission of Zondervan Publishing House. Verses marked TLB are taken from the THE LIVING BIBLE, © 1971 by Tyndale House Publishers, Wheaton, IL. Used by permission. All rights reserved.

Text © 1999 Rebecca A. Egbert
Illustrations © 1999 Concordia Publishing House
Published by Concordia Publishing House
3558 S. Jefferson Avenue, St. Louis, MO 63118-3968

Manufactured in China

All rights reserved. No part of this publication may be reproduced, stored in a retrieval system, or transmitted, in any form or by any means, electronic, mechanical, photocopying, recording, or otherwise, without the prior written permission of Concordia Publishing House.

2   3   4   5   6   7   8   9   10   08   07   06   05   04   03   02   01   00